Bachelor's Buttons

Bachelor's Buttons

Poems by

David Southward

© 2020 David Southward. All rights reserved.
This material may not be reproduced in any form, published,
reprinted, recorded, performed, broadcast,
rewritten or redistributed without
the explicit permission of David Southward.
All such actions are strictly prohibited by law.

Cover design by Shay Culligan

ISBN: 978-1-950462-65-0

Kelsay Books Inc.

kelsaybooks.com

502 S 1040 E, A119
American Fork, Utah 84003

Acknowledgments

Thanks to the editors of the journals, anthologies, and websites in which the following poems first appeared:

Ariel Anthology: "The Gay Man's Ex-Girlfriend"
Bramble: "Mayflower Compact" and "Mustache Magic"
Gyroscope Review: "The Competition"
Light: "Lessons of Etymology"
Loves Affairs at the Villa Nelle: "Lake Michigan Inlet"
The Lyric: "Bachelor's Buttons" and "The Book-Club Enchantress"
Maria W. Faust Sonnet Contest Winners: "In Defense of Formal Poetry" (2018 Laureate's Choice) and "The Chef at Home" (2019 Regional Winner)
Millwork: "Whose Hands"
The New Verse News: "Ex-Olympian"
Peacock Journal: "Dürer's Self-Portrait at 26" and "In Paradise with Jane Austen"
Poets to Come Anthology: "Walt Whitman, Are You Watching?"
The St. Sebastian Review: "Gargoyles"
Stoneboat Literary Journal: "Lost in Kandinsky"
THINK: "Communion Song," "Who's Afraid?", and "Working (It) Out with Teena Marie"

Unsplendid: "Postcards from Mom's Condo"

Van Gogh Dreams: "39 Vincents"

Verse-Virtual: "After Regrets" and "Leaving the Palmer House Hotel"

Voices on the Wind: "How to Calm Your Beagle in a Storm" and "Vision at Ojo Caliente Spa"

Wisconsin Fellowship of Poets Museletter: "Seven Ways of Looking at Yourself"

This book would not be possible without the inspiration of friends, family, students, and colleagues too numerous to mention. For encouragement and critical feedback, I am especially grateful to Steven Monte, Marilyn Taylor, the Hartford Avenue Poets, and the closest of all readers, Geoff Trotier.

Contents

I

Gargoyles	17
Macramé	18
Boys on Bikes	19
Sanibel Survivors	22
Dürer's Self-Portrait at 26	24
Kissing Contest at the A.P. Reading	25
Synchronized Diving	27
Postcards from Mom's Condo	28

II

The Gay Man's Ex-Girlfriend	33
Who's Afraid?	34
A Boyfriend's Breakfast	36
Bitter Eggplant	37
Throwing Out Your Amaryllis	38
Leaving the Palmer House Hotel	39
Bi-Poetic	40
Nipples of Men	41
Whose Hands	42
Rejection on the Oak Leaf Trail	43

III

Mayflower Compact	47
Vision at Ojo Caliente Spa	49
39 Vincents	51
Wallace at the Office	52
Bosch Triptych	54
Bachelor's Buttons	55
Letter to Mark Doty	56
Lost in Kandinsky	59
The Competition	60
Working (It) Out with Teena Marie	62

IV

After Regrets	65
Ex-Olympian	66
The Book-Club Enchantress	68
Lessons of Etymology	69
Walt Whitman, Are You Watching?	71
Guardian of the Bride	74
Seven Ways of Looking at Yourself	76
In Defense of Formal Poetry	77
How to Calm Your Beagle in a Storm	78
Raspberry Harvest	80
Communion Song	81

V

Reminder	85
Mustache Magic	86
Reading Marlowe's Biography on the Deck	87
Plans for My Reincarnation	88
In Paradise with Jane Austen	89
Lake Michigan Inlet	90
Knots	91
The Chef at Home	93
The Night We Put Tchaikovsky On	94
Groom's Song	96

I

Gargoyles

Straining their necks
to feel the sunlight, God's
prisoners bare their teeth.
They curse the architects
whose spires
they dwell beneath.

Across their backs
run troughs of stone, designed
to catch and filter rain
through their open mouths. Shrieks
of bubbled,
filthy pain

are sometimes heard
by children playing below,
who look up and ask why
God breeds such ugly birds
and what
they signify.

The boy who knows
has never thrown a ball
as far or straight as others.
He daydreams—unlike those
athletes
who, as brothers,

work in a team—
and stands apart to watch
their triumphs taking shape,
with his shoulders hunched
in thought,
his mouth agape.

Macramé

Mom enrolled
in an evening class,
botched a butterfly on wood block
and muscled through
hours
of gnarled yarn
dangling from a driftwood stake,
before giving up.
But you,
Dad, discovered
you had a knack for macramé.
Looping her leftover
jute
round a hook
in the ceiling, you braided coarse
helixes that split—
tapering
into bored corners
of mahogany (shelves for our unlit
incense and potted
Dieffenbachia);
then tied it all together
with a graduate's tassel. Your multilevel
Eiffels filled our house
with math
done strictly for pleasure.
From the carpet I salvaged scraps
to make a noose
or lasso.

Boys on Bikes

Boys on bikes meet up
at the trail head, circle
each other vulture-like,
then churn the pedals
hard to take their place
in a many-brothered
chain. The lake
they circumnavigate
is a diamond-fingered
flashing in the trees;
they slink beside it
shaded, serpentine.

Boys on bikes grind
gravel in their rubber
tread, spit stones out
like smithy sparks
in the woodland ditch,
and when they lean
into a turn, catch
flak in their spokes
with a *ting*. Shifting,
they synchronize gears
and tighten the wires
of their hamstrings.

Boys on bikes take an in-
cline standing up, just hug
that goddamned hill un-
til it peaks and levels
off; then they glide
in their momentum

down the sloping
easy side. Feet poised,
their rotors tick-a-tick
like shiny insects
in the meadow—a buzz
that's joy to make.

Boys on bikes won't brake
for folks in their way;
they close the distance,
overtake a slowpoke
family with a hollered
"On your left!"—breeze by
like fire engines
in a convoy. Only
the weaklings flinch
at daddy's curse, or dread
the witchcraft sting
of mama's mumbling.

Boys on bikes coast in
to the ice cream stand
sidesaddle, dismount
with a one-hand hop
and line their wheels up
in the fence slats.
They drop change
for cones—lick them fast
as the sun melts, race
for the open bathroom
to slick their hair
with cold tap water.

Boys on bikes are mute
while flying single-file
in forest light about
the god they exercise.
His gruff embrace
can crush the individual
in us; to speak of it
embarrasses. Enough
to wear him out
with a daily breathing—
in the regimental motion
of a neighborhood machine.

Sanibel Survivors

Thrown ashore by the backhoe
action of spent waves, the live coquinas
lie stunned. A homing instinct
tips them on their sides; they wriggle,
wedging their polished bodies
down through slick sands
that close behind them. I have come

this morning to pore absently
over drenched and dried remains
of pulverized seashells. Stepping cautious
as on a bed of nails, I stoop to pick up
calico scallops: purple-streaked
and strewn along the beach like lockets
a thief has unhinged. The sun

comes up behind a prickly band
of terns—eyeing the horizon
with fierce black brows, orange bills
sniffing the wind. Phalanx-like,
they guard the entrance to a shoal
that only now, at low tide,
floats near enough the surface
to be walked on. My bare feet

follow its corrugated floor,
as if to read the algorithms
graphed there in Braille. Farther out
than I've ever been, in the tide pool's
shimmering habitat, I find
the burnished, broth-gold armor
of a fighting conch. Bending to observe
its eyes, bobbing on twin antennae,

I notice algae billowing like green hair
from a gash cut deep in its hull.
Yards beyond, where the sandbar

rises out of the Gulf, I spot another,
then another: all burrowing out of the earth
to start the workday's shuffling dance.
In the quiet of their kingdom, Time
slows down; each snail contestant drags
into the sun his wobbly crown.

Dürer's Self-Portrait at 26

He catches you in the act
of looking—
at the cleft fruit of his lips,

at the insidiously tangled
wavelets of
cornsilk hair cascading

to his shoulder. A silvery link
of rope
secures his cape, drawn taut

against the luminous hues
of lean flesh.
You think, here is a man

who knows what he wants,
who can face
the sun of his own pride

fearlessly. And isn't that
a telltale mark
of genius? Never to blink,

squint, or look away
from the blaze
and lose oneself in shadows?

Kissing Contest at the A.P. Reading

I left the bar with Marco and the girls
to walk the beach path back to our hotel.
The night was lush—a black sea frothed with winds
that cooled the sand. Kicking our sandals off,
we stumbled, partly drunk, past isles of grass,
dance tunes thumping in our chests. Not tired
yet knowing we'd need sleep to score exams
the next day, we dragged our heels—as though time
would prove elastic in this paradise
of English teachers far from school and home.
Inspired, Kathleen clapped playfully and asked,
"Who's the best kisser here?" No better way
to find out than by kissing one another
pronto, she urged, in twos—a mock pop quiz
we'd give ourselves to make the night last longer.
Who could refuse her smile of impish glee?
I joined her for the first round, letting all
my inhibitions melt against her lips—
not from desire so much as vanity
(curse of the insecure): a lingering itch
to prove that, although gay, I was a man.
As if on cue, I pressed my conscious hands
firmly against the taut arch of her back—
in imitation of the screen embrace
I'd seen a million times. Her gentle gasp
and murmur of approval gave me strength
to face the next contestant: Betsy, queen
of gangly, farm-bred boys' rebellious hearts.
A sultry former track star, she'd skipped class
to meet her girlfriends for a cigarette
under the bleachers. Could I light a spark
in one so wild? Clasping her by the waist
I felt her pull me closer—found the taste

of beer and menthol blended in her breath.
The cool shock of saliva as our lips
parted with a smack, braced me for round three.
My pulse sped; thinking uncontrollably
of where Kathleen's experiment had led,
I turned to Marco looming in the dark.
Husband and father, athlete, writer, flirt
whose olive skin, black hair, and jawline scruff
made clear why Troy could never get enough
of Hector—he was my opponent now.
I watched him scan the ground like frightened prey
and, overcome by his mute bashfulness,
assured him, "We don't have to." But he raised
his eyes to mine and mumbled, "It's okay."
It's okay: he would let me cross the line
I'd drawn between myself and men like him—
pushing aside all fear of being hurt
by towel-snapping critics in the gym
to kiss the prickly source of my distress
and be kissed back! I closed my eyes, too stunned
to feel the blood come roaring in my ears
as our lips touched. When voices had begun
to reach us, and the atmosphere to crack
with raucous laughter, faintly I could hear
Kathleen, squealing and clutching at my shirt
to help me understand: "You won! You won!"

Synchronized Diving

two men
at the apogee
pivot and tuck
folding their limbs
into each other's
silhouette
they somersault
as one
in slow motion
no eye contact
to encourage
the solvent
nemesis
deep accomplices
splitting the water
curled toes
simultaneously
swallowed by
the cool surface

like missiles
of silence
tipping earthward
instinctively
ankle-locked
in a free fall
tumbling
symmetrically
the men share
a twin pact
total defiance of
undisciplined
deviation
they finish
with prayer hands
muscular wishes
submerged
nothing more than
ripples

Postcards from Mom's Condo

On either side of the drive, guardian palms
stand in islands of bleached stone.
Their fronds fan terra cotta pots
that tilt toward the morning sun,
spilling fictional oils
of amber chalk—
their mouths ajar,
a lizard in one.

*

What wakes me is not the incessant clack
of vertical blinds in the guest room,
but the periodic *who, who* of doves
filtering in to ease the brain
from hebetude.
I turn in the sheets,
remembering this
is White Haven Lane.

*

Brown-breasted ladies meet at the pool, to hang
on foam noodles and weigh in
on convalescent homes, each other's migraines,
mutual funds that eat their dividends.
The fittest of them does her laps
on tiptoe—fifty-some,
to and fro
in the shallow end.

*

Behold Michael, the Chico's designer
who took me for sushi at a place called Blu,
walking his Chihuahua, Lulu
past Mom's lanai. I wave, but instead
he greets the Frauen who bow
to Lulu—spotting his work
in their rayon skirts,
Hibiscus Red.

    *

Sun's on my back. I run beside the marsh
where palmettos soak, watch the bike path
spool on my shadow self
without accretion. Cars race by, tire peelings
roll to the shoulder.
One foot prints
an anthill.
What are my feelings?

    *

Mom sweeps beach salts from the outer stairs
as I write postcards in my condo Zen.
So evenly does the ceiling fan
wag on its axle, so clear is the blot
my beverage makes on a napkin,
that I come to wonder
whether I am here
or not.

II

The Gay Man's Ex-Girlfriend

After their split, she'd turn up in his dreams
as if all was forgiven. They'd huddle together
pressing bubbles from bread dough, or picnic
on the shoreline rocks of her beloved Maine
and converse in the resting brain's birdsong
of nonsense. A decade passed; her visits
became less frequent. She seemed to hover
at the perimeter of a circle anxiously drawn
around him, her face serious. If she spoke,
it was in phrases so cryptic and piecemeal
he would wake up clawing at each word,
an Oedipus with a riddle. Now, if she comes
at all, it's to stare at him with the white-eyed
impassivity of a sarcophagus. Hard to tell
what she means by it—just loitering there
with nothing more to say; no longer herself
but a residue that won't dissolve. He wonders
if it's her purpose to block the passageway
between worlds, or maybe to hold the door.

Who's Afraid?

Hearing the news that Edward Albee died,
I pictured myself at twenty-one—in school,
taking my girlfriend to see *Who's Afraid
of Virginia Woolf?* A guilt-tormented couple,
George and Martha, waged war on the stage
with hints of a son they'd damaged (or made up),

showing how love itself was half made up
of violent wishes. Though no one died,
watching their marriage blow apart on stage
was thrilling. Like cadets fresh out of school,
we saw ourselves in the play's younger couple,
the newlyweds—knowing we'd be afraid

to put our love to the test, though not afraid
enough. For soon the manhood I'd made up
would start to peel; the picture-perfect couple
our parents believed we'd be some day, died—
and she and I moved on to graduate school.
My mask ripped off, I welcomed life's next stage

not knowing that I'd reached its cruelest age:
the baffling twenties—identity all frayed
from trying to keep one's broth of passions cool.
A boyfriend whose good looks could not make up
for curt, unkind remarks, left me red-eyed.
And love? A firefly no one could cup whole.

I studied literature's most illustrious couples,
surprised to learn how much was left offstage.
Albee was gay; Virginia Woolf had died
by her own hand; most writers were afraid

of people seeing through what they'd made up.
Classics our teachers rave about in school

come nowhere near the shock of that first school
of the real—where couple after stumbling couple
gropes on a darkened set, their minds made up
to play a love scene never before staged.
Each gets undressed, thinking, *I'm not afraid,
are you?*—and wonders if the mood has died.

Imagine a stage: after the applause has died,
where couples have fought, surrendered, or made up
and school's let out for good. Now enter (afraid).

A Boyfriend's Breakfast

Remember how you used to bake me bread?
Our rented rooms above the hardware store
would fill up with that scent. Though we were poor
(with years of unpaid scholarship ahead)
you took fierce pride in how your man was fed.
Each loaf was cradled from the oven door
and held up to my nose. By God, you swore
I'd fatten like a sultan once we wed.

Time taught us, though, that bread could taste more sweet
to slaves than sultans—servants who grow thin
with expectation of when *they* will eat,
who bite their tongues while toughening their skin.
"No one can live on appetite alone,"
your bread knife might have warned as it went in.

Bitter Eggplant

Astonishing to look at in their basket,
like blanched plums or lavender tomatoes,
these Asian market fruits defied the nose—
with skin so bland, no bloodhound could unmask it.

The farmer's daughter warned us not to buy them.
Her caveat was good enough for me
(if she couldn't stand the taste, then how would we?),
but you were undeterred and had to try them.

Sliced into quarters, salted, leached, sautéed
until their flabby innards gleamed and burst
against the tongue like rancid lemonade,
your beauties proved unwilling to be eaten.
You threw them out, conceding they were cursed.
Some natures are impossible to sweeten.

Throwing Out Your Amaryllis

You wooed me with a rugged Valentine:
an amaryllis bulb, a pot, and soil—
and doing my damnedest not to seem disloyal,
I drenched it in a window's faint sunshine.

Within a week it sprouted silent tongues
that stretched up inch by inch and thickened green.
Somewhere inside their widening throat, unseen,
were my bashful flower's embryonic blooms.

I waited. The leaf-stalks spread, but still no sign
of a budding amaryllis could be found
in the pitiless, white, fibrous crease they made.

Your gift of love began to seem malign.
With recklessness at heart—and scarce a sound—
I chucked that barren flower in the shade.

Leaving the Palmer House Hotel

Up at seven, fresh-eyed, morning-stubbled,
you chug a mocha java in the lobby, pause to admire
gilt peacocks in profile
on Mr. Tiffany's imperial doors, then glide out
on the doorman's smile. You'd tip
a hat if you had one—you're that elated

to be thrust into the skyscraped, sunrise-brushed
December workday, where Carl Sandburg's citizens
still pound by thousands
across Chicago's shuddering bridges.
In each face you see a time-clock
stalking its fate—a human becoming
its incandescent, dreamed-of self; God's celebrity.

You lift and lengthen your stride, shake the need
for a companion to confide in
under freezing canopies, and eavesdrop
on the legions of petitioners
who flirt and quarrel with smooth plastic
circuitry in their ears.
Delayed at the corner, you look up

just as that priestess topping the Board of Trade,
nickeled Ceres, turns a cool pink—
and the sensation travels all the way
down to your karmic feet.

Bi-Poetic

There's a part of me that can't resist
the muscles of a formalist
        and part that craves the more supple
            curves of free verse.

I'm half a stickler for precision,
half a fool for Dionysian
        energies that disrupt
            poetic structures. Is that so wrong?

When two devotions alternate
in one man, how can just one mate
        answer the changing vibrations
            of his being? This is hardly a question

of "orientation": one's nose is prone
to fall for perfume or cologne,
        and words come from every direction
            to kiss the ear. Dogmatists who believe

we poets should be forced to choose
a métier . . . screw them! I refuse
        to sacrifice half of my natural inclinations.
            In fact, I'm just perverse enough

to merge my Hyde and Jekyll measures
into a mutant line, whose pleasures
        bypass and transcend
            our literary categories

altogether. To hell with critics—
I'll compose *hermaphroditics:*
        love songs to human beings
            of unfathomed persuasion.

Nipples of Men

Not quite tits
or teats, just pectoral points
of interest: a torso's eyes
caught staring
at the beach; pinpricks
disturbing a taut Oxford's
cotton; coppery beacons
appearing through sheer Ts.
Aureoles varying
like fingerprints—in diameter
from clamshell to dime, in tint
from plum to pink—each
with its own punch code
of goosebumps. Sensitive
to the barest hints
of coolness in blood
or air flow, they shrivel
like witches
in water, hibernate
in whorls of hair. Whether hubs
of ecstasy or indifference,
bashful paps or rubbery
dugs—pierced, thick
as toothpaste—they are
unmistakably a man's
most naked part. Impractical
glands, sore reminders
of what he can't give,
they are the clenched petals
of him—harmless and endearing
as embarrassments
he pretends
aren't happening.

Whose Hands

"Whose hand is *that?*" blurts one
of six grown men in a hot tub
built for two, who've chugged
enough beer by the pitcherful
to tug at their waistband strings,
finger and undo the inner knots
holding up each other's trunks,
and hurl those peeled skins
too far into outer darkness
to be retrieved. Bubbles break
against my chin as I sink further
in, wondering, *Whose hands
are these*—attaching to my calves
like starfish in the camouflage
of beige and languid flesh?
And are my toes making their way
in answer to the inner thigh
of the dimpled rascal
facing me, arriving at last
at that weightlessness, his shy
and billowing anemone?
He smiles across a screen
of percolation; someone catching on
in bursts of chlorinated laughter
cries, "Hands out of the water!"
and up they come: his silver palms
still glistening with thievery.
He gets away with it scot-free,
but oh, how I could throttle
the rat that squealed on him—
my privateering knave, whose pair
of treasure-seeking hands
I'd gladly sink again to fill.

Rejection on the Oak Leaf Trail

Shirtless
he floats into view,
the last man I'd expect:

a prince
in wire spectacles,
who's brandishing a net.

"What are you after?" I ask.
(Wretched flirt!)
He turns from the shrub,

mutters simply, "Butterflies"
and sifts me with
those eyeglass eyes.

III

Mayflower Compact

In Provincetown, the liberating home
of hippies, artisans, and lesbians,
a traveler hears the call of possibility.
Drag queens sparkle on Commercial Street
as they hawk their evening shows; tourists gawk
at pinks and blues commingling in the sky
as wildly as in gallery watercolors;
and hairy-legged men, in leather chaps
and beaded underwear, trade recipes
their darling aunts inscribed on index cards.

How frightening possibility must have seemed
to those who congregated on these shores
for the first time: the buckled, bonneted ones
blown from green Virginia further north
than any dreamed their God would let them go.
Signing their names, they made a covenant
never to swerve from His eternal laws—
as if, in time, they might incline to do so.

I understand that contract only now,
on board a ferry reeling Bostonward
despite the captain's warning of "rough seas,"
as she rises to a peak, then dips and slams
against a wave, her windows filling up
with spume, with sky, with spume, with sky—no rest
from her emetic rock-a-bye. A smell
of rancid vinegar ensues, a qualm
I tried to swallow with my Dramamine
returns, and, like my pilgrim forefathers,
unmoored from any steady, certain ground
in white-capped undulations and riptide,
I mumble to myself some anchoring words

to stabilize and orient my mind:

The lure of possibility is fine
for those who know by instinct where they stand,
but those like me—unsteady in their souls
and coasting far from anywhere they'd planned—
must constantly remember to look back
at what they've left, think why, and with their hand
set down the steadfast traces of their will,
before the impulse casually subsides
or founders in a wave of seasickness.

I, the undersigned, do swear to this.

Vision at Ojo Caliente Spa

The aesthetician leads me down a hall
with many doors, to one reserved for me
and asks me to disrobe. Light as a seed
I slip inside the table's cotton pocket—
tucked there by the wedging of her hands
beneath my ribcage, thighs, and ticklish calves.
She wraps my neck and feet with hot washcloths—
so hot the muscles soften as I sink
into a mummified state. Eyelids sealed
with moistened petals, I breathe in the scent
of eucalyptus whipped into emollients.
She spreads the granule butter with both hands,
finger-painting my forehead, cheeks, and chin
in looping figure eights until my features
disappear. Impressions bubble up
through pores in time, the sloughed identities
vacationers try on: Georgia O'Keefe
standing nude by a mud bath, her lover
molding her in the desert's mauve and tan
with a wood spatula. Parched in the sun,
her face is an exfoliating mask
with holes for eyes, its whiteness camouflaged
in lizard skin. At dusk the fluttering
wings of a hawk across the mesa's ridge
remind her of a charred black crucifix
the missionaries left on the horizon.
Beyond it, Taos: a juniper's green fan,
where an eastern heiress wed a Pueblo prince
who promised her a pink adobe house
and laid its molten walls with his bare hands.

In dream-speech she remembers what they said:
*Follow the spiral stairway. Feel the pith
of being in your body's sacred lake,
while fingers on a shimmering guitar
reanimate the dormant reservoir.*

39 Vincents

What was it he kept seeing
  in the barber's mirror
    propped against a basin?

Each time the vulpine face
  emerged from its field
    of intensity—all brow

and cheekbone and raked hair—
  did it momentarily become
    less secret? The fur hat

changed for the straw;
  leather collar now cinched,
    now unbuttoned:

so many hours spent fussing
  with Parisian accoutrements,
    before the inchoate

denizen could rise
  to the surface, flaunting a beard
    of wet copper.

Is it only through ritual
  that such images come?
    The thumbs of a shaman

daubing a clay mask;
  the deity glimpsed
    in hawk's plumage.

Wallace at the Office

Immaculately dressed, he comes and goes
without a word. A wall of steel grey wool
advancing past your desk at nine, at five,

he smells of soap flakes and pistachios;
a comb's gone freshly through his silver hair.
He'll glance your way, but never with the eyes

behind the eyes, as it were—that ulterior gaze
so visibly preoccupied with neither
your opinions nor your incidental life,

but with the burbling of some vaguer fantasy.
Women despise him. Men stand clear.
The rumor circulating that he's queer

belies the simmering quality of his rage
for solitude . . . those stifling afternoons
he shuts his door, flexing his authority

as a porcupine its camouflage of quills.
For years we had no inkling he was writing
poems in that privacy he requires:

whole volumes, hinting at intelligences
wider than any underwriter's. Stunned
to discover one secondhand, I like to thumb

its brittle leaves before I fall asleep,
not pretending to fully comprehend
the meaning of its surreptitious smiles

or flight path of its philosophic thoughts—
cooing and teasing apart the quandaries
of existence with a feathered edge. I've come

to think of him as an artist, and furthermore
to think: an artist's gift is not compassion
for strangers, but compassion for one's own

more strange, profane, unmitigated self—
freak exile in an echoing rotunda,
defenseless against an avalanche of claims.

Bosch Triptych

At one end stands God in the orchard of bliss,
imparting to Adam the gift of a wife;
far opposite, mayhem in Hell's dank abyss
completes the Dutch master's partition of life.
Between them, a theme park of lewdness invites
all eyes to the Garden of Earthly Delights.

Here people cavort with the freedom of beasts—
in handstands, on horseback, from hollowed-out rinds
of pink melon; some bend over strawberry feasts
while flashing their wildflower-sprouting behinds!
It's nature's absurdity—raised to new heights
by art in the Garden of Earthly Delights.

Where leopard and lobster, opossum and shark,
in league with the camel and clamshell and boar,
parade like the stock of some mutinous ark
through circus grounds, bowing to Noah no more.
Wild creatures lay claim to unlimited rights
when roaming the Garden of Earthly Delights.

Dancers in covens raise totems on biers;
beaks graze the lips of insatiable flirts;
teams of explorers, in glass bathyspheres,
ride nude on a pond; and a tumbler inverts
while squeezing a seed-pod between his strong thighs.
(Can anyone guess what this folly implies?)

The painter's conviction flames out in full craze
from each swollen bud, berry, tendril, and squash:
as long as man lives, as hard as he prays,
the pulp of his origins will not wash off,
and art is the struggle on warm, wet nights
to give up the Garden of Earthly Delights.

Bachelor's Buttons

I waited for a garden god
to show me where to tear the sod,
but grew impatient, once I saw
my garden had no border law.

In virgin beds that hugged the fence
I carried out experiments
to see which cultivated guest
would flourish in the plain Midwest.

I tried the princely, spiraled rose
and watched it blacken as it froze.
My calloused greeting proved too chilly
for the righteous Easter lily.

Sickened by their own perfume,
my hyacinths would droop too soon;
the green hydrangeas had no clue
how to achieve their promised blue.

Accepting the mistakes one makes
before a transplant fully takes,
while trying to regain the ease
of nature within boundaries,

I saw the bachelor's buttons crop
up by surprise—and blue buds pop
like cufflink studs, with purple eyes
that met the fire of the sky's
and drank from roots now just as deep
as promises a man can keep.

Letter to Mark Doty

We've never met. I was still a teen
   in '84, while you'd gone in pursuit
      of phantoms, signaling through the fog

of Castro Street. Men whose damp shirts
   swung from their belt loops
      fastened you in a trance,

and you followed: a fearless pagan
   consenting to bear witness
      to a plague. The dying changed you

the way that Marsyas was changed
   by Apollo—some punishing god
      turning the costume of your skin

inside out, until even the whiskey breath
   of beggars would scorch and sting
      your suit of nerves. Empathy

comes readily to the inconsolable;
   the ones who sidestep grief
      remain immune. Death visited us

on *Newsweek* covers: a gaunt screen star
   escorted to his limousine
      through the white-hot sniper's glare

of flash bulbs, as a towering myth
   of manhood shuddered and gave way.
      For a young man still at war

with his identity, that indelible linkage
   of rapture with dread
      was fatal. It froze the seed

of my generation, driving instinct
   underground. I felt the symptoms
      on the first night I went home

with a stranger, simply to relieve
   a long pent-up anticipation
      of The One. After a fumbling affair

of sofa cushions and crumpled jeans,
   when he'd left the darkened room
      to wash himself, I was overcome

with panic. Why did he take so long?
   Was he planning to come back
      to kill me? That's how nervously

we courted in the days of a millennial
   curfew. One would approach
      the temple of another's body

like a vandal, half-expecting to be seized
   in mid-disgrace. I learned to hide
      inside the waxed armor

of my physique, unable to work
   the jammed mechanism
      of the mouth. It took me twenty years.

The day I bought your book
   in Chicago, when all of Boys' Town
     lay hushed under settled snow,

the sidewalks glistened at sunset
   like tropical gelato—every corner
     heaped with pink, hibernal fruit.

I saw in the crisscross of footprints
   a scrapbook of trysts, and discovered
     in your rhapsodies, a terminus:

This is where we meet, the pages
   whispered, nudging me
     toward an invisible labyrinth

of loss, wherein every surge
   and flicker of desire softly turns
     into the only life

worth saving. Ethereal guide
   and enthusiast, replenish me
     with words, teach me to dance

like a gentleman with a rose
   between his teeth, ink on his hands.

Lost in Kandinsky

Start anywhere: a purple curlicue
bisecting an arc
of barbed wire, suspended in sky-blue
and yellow nebulae. Plunge with your eye
through vortices
of paper cut-outs, whirling ostrich feathers
and stenciled mitochondria. Golf tees, neckties,
succulent speared olives
orbiting rainbows
of wrinkled cellophane: the whole fiery glitter
leading inevitably to that red throb
of war in the corner. With its tangled kites, its rotors
spewing ribbons of hemoglobin, the mandala's
big-bang windmill
inhales all but one charioteer
who escapes. See where he's headed: Psychedelia,
where polka dots float
like embryos—through the permeable
stained-glass membranes
of a heaven
with no vanishing point.

The Competition

Word spread fast: the steering committee,
eager to launch Chicago's Exposition,
would need a symbol for the city's
worldlier ambition—

a structure to exceed men's dreams,
to rival Eiffel's miracle in Paris.
Contestants sketched out countless schemes.
In Pittsburgh, young George Ferris,

fresh from a railway bridge design,
passed up a night of euchre with his friends
to study Eiffel's graceful lines
through a magnifying lens.

The tower awed the engineer.
Seeing it as the bridge of earth and sky,
he wondered: what extreme frontier
remained for him to try?

He undid bolts; rotated beams;
changed angles; altered curvature and weight.
Teased by a stateliness that seemed
too perfect to translate,

he spun the figure—let a weird
chaos detach the observation decks
and loop them. In his mind appeared
a structure more complex:

a wheel of dangling terraces,
revolving from the crowd-packed fairground queues
to summits—prized, like Paris's,
for panoramic views.

The judges praised his sense of fun,
spoke of a showman's grit backed up with science—
and gravitation overcome
with something like defiance.

Working (It) Out with Teena Marie

She whoops into my ears; the whole gym whirls.
I turn the volume up to shush the *clink*
of my elliptical machine. Like joyous squirrels

her scatted oohs and shoop-pops leap in sync
with youthful biorhythms now gone slack.
And she's been dead how long? Five years, I think,

letting the iPod's witchcraft take me back
to summers in Ft. Myers: bored, sixteen,
racing my bike down streets whose hot shellac

exuded waves of harsh, phenolic steam.
Clipped to my shorts, a tape player filled my head
with pop sensations. Warnings to come clean

pursued me through desire's infrared.
I saw the manly shadows moving nearer;
I pounded harder, like a thoroughbred.

These boys who curl their biceps in the mirror:
what are they after? Strength won't make them freer
pullers of Beauty's drawstring. Do they fear her

because they sense how good it feels to be her?
Fanned by an AC vent, I bounce and hurtle
past them through time—a stationary skier

for whom the trails of memory unfurl
this chorus, like a plaintive reprimand:
I just want to be your lovergirl.

IV

After Regrets

for Steven Monte

As a younger man I dreamed of writing prose
whose cadences would inundate the heart,
warming those sensibilities that froze
when poets stripped the music from their art.

Now that in middle years I've switched to verse
and left those storytelling dreams behind,
my youth's ambition lingers like a curse
in language too flamboyantly designed

to overwhelm. That's why I look to you,
old friend, whose practiced ear for pitch is true,
to help me rein in my insubordinate line;

I trust that you'll point out what's overdone,
and that in time your subtleties will run
some clarifying water through my wine.

Ex-Olympian

Oscar Pistorius
bolts for the glorious
gold
on his boomerang heels.
Crowds at the starting line
gasp as Pretoria's
champion
gallantly kneels.

Off goes a pistol!
The crowd leaps, uproarious,
watching the sprinter
break free . . .
scarcely imagining
what a victorious
marksman
the sprinter could be.

Now that his haste
has occasioned the goriest
halt
to a Valentine's Day,
and he's mustered the sorriest
look that a boyfriend
of any dead girl
could display,

will Oscar explain
how he found it uxorious—
minding a woman's
appeals?

When the crowd stands aghast
at how feeble his story is,
Oscar may know
how she feels.

The Book-Club Enchantress

She'd seat us at her table with a smile
as warm as any queen's. Like clumsy knights
we tried to imitate her polished style;
our cheese knives clinked against her dainty plates.
The evening's intellectual delights
were strengthened by allegiance to her dream
of friendship. To us that's how it seemed.

Behind closed doors, she felt herself alone:
our loose-knit bonds and casual sympathy
would never match the fervor of her own.
The loyalty we pledged was too low-key.
When someone needed comfort, it was she
who tended to the business. No one knew
how desperately she wanted comfort, too.

She'd have to teach us. With one crisp note
informing us how deeply hurt she'd been,
we were cast adrift. Nothing else we wrote—
apologies, expressions of chagrin—
could reach the stubborn heart she had walled in.
That Old World trope, *la belle dame sans merci,*
had shown us just how current she could be.

Lessons of Etymology

How does a name become a word—
the syllables which once referred
to someone, doubling as a term
that spreads like an infectious germ?

Did rumors swirl when ladies danced
in Amelia Bloomer's skirtless pants?
Or scandal graze the second skin
that Monsieur Léotard waltzed in?

Maybe it's praise for work done right:
high fives for Daniel Fahrenheit;
our amped-up thanks (it's only fair)
to dear André-Marie Ampère.

If pedigree can feed a trend,
the Earl of Sandwich's won't end!
A vintage chic is half the fun
of dressing like Lord Cardigan.

Brand names, as a general rule,
will stick like Rudolf Diesel's fuel,
or sink in with the warm blub-blub
of a Jacuzzi Brothers tub.

Scofflaws who drive their towns berserk
(like Charles Boycott—what a jerk!)
get branded, too. It did the trick
for ranchman Samuel Maverick.

But fame can take unheard-of forms.
Few wagered on the steel hailstorms
of Henry Shrapnel. None foresaw
the fate of Colonel Lynch's law.

Best to supply a pressing want,
as Louis Braille did with his font;
or die in shadow—like the debt
we trace to Etienne Silhouette.

Walt Whitman, Are You Watching?

O Walt, if you could wake to see
our sex-besotted century—
and from your grave, with widening eyes
survey its soulless enterprise—
what would you make of DVDs
in which men copulate in threes?
of college girls who flash their gams
to sociopaths through dorm-room cams?
Would situations so perverse
receive your blessing—or a curse?

The adolescent iPod teems
with auto-tuned erotic dreams,
with rap songs that abuse the rhymes
for "bitch" and "booty" countless times;
while aging men (to whom the young
might turn to right a world gone wrong)
look backward in their search for truth
to the erections of their youth!
Walt, tell us, is that what you meant
by honoring our embodiment?

The cameramen who keep their wits
while dueling vamps adjust their tits
objectify the working class
to kick some rival network's ass.
It seems that our democracy's
no match for such hypocrisies.
Now that ratings rise with pulses,
hotness rules (or so a poll says);
only those can get elected
who've been sexually selected.
Help us, Walt, to understand:
what happened to your promised land?

Newsmen, sporting whitened smiles,
flush out squirming pedophiles
so craftily, there seems no way
to tell the predator from prey.
It's not injustice or oppression
that's exposed, but indiscretion—
as if the nation's only care
was who did what to whom and where.
Can poetry make any sense,
O Captain, of our prurience?
Shall masters of the cell-phone arts
(who publicize their private parts
to strangers querying "how hung?")
presume the body electric sung?

I'd like to think, if you came back,
your verse would take a different tack:
you'd yawp at your Americans
to tie their hair back into buns,
button up their loosened trousers,
save the goodies for their spouses.
But face it, Walt, we know that you
were something of a pervert, too.
You'd loiter round a woodland pool
where bucks swam shirtless after school,
and when they scampered out of reach,
you'd cruise for comrades at the beach.
Odds are, today you'd join the herd
that rolls down Broadway Ave., chauffeured
and add to your long list of joys
a troupe of naked singing boys.

Maybe we should just embrace
the truth we find so hard to face:
that underneath our Puritan
façade of moral cleanliness,
we've always had an eye for fun,
and spectacle's what we do best.

Who cares if learned astronomers
predict our expedition's failure:
let's send a rocket to the stars
with essence of our genitalia

smeared in stripes of DNA,
so startled aliens can tell
the universe that we said "Hey!"
It won't be calamus they smell

(if they have means olfactory)
but something gutsier, more crass
we picked up absent-mindedly
while tramping through your *Leaves of Grass*.

Guardian of the Bride

Hanging from a rafter
in my sister's attic loft:
the brand-new bridal dress
she's dying to show me—
still inside a garment bag
that's femininely contoured
yet zeppelin-like, its vinyl
puffed and foamy.

My sister takes it from the hook
and lays it on the bed,
where it creases at the waist—
a matron fainting, overfed,
her seams aburst with air
she can't let go. Headless
as a dummy in de Chirico,
she preys upon an archetypal dread.

Reaching for a zipper
tucked inside a furtive sheath,
my sister strips the schoolmarm
of her bodice;
the gown within is trim
and complicated, with a web
of silk brocade to snare
the bosom of a goddess.

If only love were tailor-made.
A bride's dress is her dream
of exaltation, lit with all
her starward thoughts.

The vessel that it's shuttled in
must guard against the flames
and have the buoyancy
to match an astronaut's.

Seven Ways of Looking at Yourself

A student of experience.
A victim of desire.
Believer in the cold, hard truth.
Habitual white liar.
The one who runs for cover.
The one who sees things through.
The double in a darkened window
thinking, "Oh, it's you."

In Defense of Formal Poetry

"This sonnet stuff is fake," my class complains:
emotion crammed unnaturally into schemes
that show how skilled a poet is at games
but not what's in his heart—his fears and dreams.
Cornered by skeptics, how can I explain
that meter is the pulse of breath and blood
beneath one's conscious ecstasy and pain,
and helps to make these feelings understood?
Or that emotion, given form, is like a flood
strengthening under pressures of design:
its surge grows more distinct—a music heard
in waves that lap and burst against the rhyme.
Form isn't fake. It's just a poet's way
to underscore what he finds hard to say.

How to Calm Your Beagle in a Storm

Begin by nestling him
between your upper thigh
and a sofa's padded arm.

When the rumbling nears
and threatens to collapse
the sky, gently fold back

his velvet earflap, squeeze
with forefinger and thumb
the tuft of silky fur

that lines the portal
to his caverned ear,
and carefully work out

its treasured scent
of barley malt
and damp blanket.

Let the rain come
and whatever remains
of daylight

in the room, go dim;
you'll feel the quivering
in his haunches

ease, tension drain
from his coiled spine
as he draws into his depths

one double-barreled breath
and vanquishes his terror
with a sigh.

Raspberry Harvest

Peer through the thatch of mint green leaves
whose downward curl, like shading eaves
edged on all sides with shredding teeth,
shelters the treasures tucked beneath.

They're hidden well. You'll have to stoop
to find them: ruby earrings, grouped
in tightknit clans of four or five.
Up close, each fruit is like a hive

of bubbled lobes, its natal plug
withdrawing as you gently tug—
your fingertips caught unawares
by the damp swab of tickly hairs.

Steady: the hands must not be rushed.
The mellow berries may be crushed
or fall to earth; the thin flesh torn;
your thumb snagged by a subtle thorn.

Meanwhile the morning sun's oblique
spotlight shines against your cheek.
The whole back yard begins to glow.
You're in arm deep. The work is slow.

Back in the house, the ice-cold purr
of water through the colander
emits a tang like uncorked wine.
The hard part's done, you think. It's time.

Communion Song

December, 1970

He's two. The solemn Christmas service
offers him nothing he can use.
He fidgets, clambers, makes mom nervous.
The resin-scented oaken pews
echo the clop-clop of the toddler,
who struts in place—a seasoned waddler—
elbowing like a lumberjack
the shirt sleeves checkered red and black.
With each wild pounce his feet grow bolder.
Dad half-proudly eyes the pup
while Mom, indignant, scoops him up.
Perched high, he gazes past her shoulder
at strangers' faces. Some fresh thrill
arrests him. Song! His legs hang still.

*

Two rows behind, a grieving widow
gives her son's hand a squeeze that says,
We'll get through this. I promise, kiddo.
He fears her strength will undo his.
Hiding his eyes' responsive stinging
with blinked attention to the singing,
he notices the little squirt
who's worn the same checked flannel shirt!
A neighbor notes it, too; she's smiling
sweetly, as if to share her joy
on seeing the young man in the boy.
He ponders, as the herd starts filing
toward the altar one by one,
whether he'd like to have a son.

*

Across the aisle, a man's distracted—
watching the widow's son pass by
out of the corner of his eye.
Why—even here—is he attracted
to younger men with coal black hair?
And can his wife be unaware
she wears the ring of an impostor?
He hates what his concealment costs her
yet with the craft of the addicted
savors his dosage. Soon their line
will reach the priest—as he, conflicted,
partakes of blessing, bread, and wine,
bowing his head, all prayer unstrung,
the starch dissolving on his tongue.

*

No one perceives the husband's trouble
except a cagey usher, who
regards it with a scratch of stubble,
knowing how much there is to do.
Knowing how all life's wished-for kisses
come down to this (whatever "this" is),
he holds the doors; he smiles and waits;
he empties the collection plates
and snuffs the candles. Wax congealing
soothes his old brain, where "Silent Night"
still circles like a satellite.
He swallows a peculiar feeling,
and bundling up, his instep sore,
leans hard against the whistling door.

v

Reminder

Who needs the romantic Rhine
or Danube, the lush Amazon
or majestic Hudson—

when behind a row of apartments
across the street, the Milwaukee River
flows soothingly

from an unexplored source
in the cold hills? Coming to life
each April, her gown of hammered metal

undulates like the skin
of your own thoughts.
Soon she will call out

to adventurers: *This way*
to the derelict and forsaken
brewery of ideas.

Mustache Magic

for Ian

When you turned nine, nobody dreamed
your party would be mustache-themed.
Guests at the door were asked to wear
adhesive strips of facial hair
and *presto*—by that artful touch
the atmosphere was changed so much!
Kids looked more sophisticated
with their muzzles groomed and shaded,
while fussing mothers' trim goatees
inspired giggles of unease.
Cousins with bushy handle-bars
stroked them like bogus Russian czars,
and uncles leered like pool sharks
(or Stalin, mocked by Groucho Marx).
When fuzz beneath your Nana's nose
sent shivers down to Papa's toes,
it made us laugh so hard the guck
that held our stickers came unstuck—
and one by one, without a sound,
mustaches fluttered to the ground!
Unfazed, we drank from mustache straws,
ate frosting shaped by mustache laws;
in perfect sync, we shared the vibe
of living as one mustached tribe.
I hope these birthday wonders stick
in your memory—and some new trick
occurs to you, when you turn ten,
to turn us into better men.

Reading Marlowe's Biography on the Deck

I picture him at Rheims: the stubbly rogue
who loved to whisper in a papist's ear
the secret of the Queen's acrostic code.
How swiftly his theatrical career
launched him on the double-agent plots
with which his nation's ruling coterie
conspired to entrap the French and Scots.

What would that man of action think of me?
My breakfast of buttered toast, marmalade
and imported coffee; the grass just mowed;
the maple, dense with seed, supplying shade
for daydreams of the ways life can unfold . . . .
Hearing the branches rustle, I look up;
a helicopter rattles in my cup.

Plans for My Reincarnation

When I come back, I won't be late
or second-guess or hesitate.
I'll know exactly what I want,
attack life like a bold savant
who will not curl into his shell
or tolerate a private hell.
I'll voice my joy and discontent,
show love without embarrassment,
pursue romance with no illusions,
jump at chances—not conclusions.

And all those things I meant to do?
When I come back, I'll follow through:
I'll study French, watch less TV,
play sports, write letters, sing on key.
My focus will be so intense,
my poetry will make more sense.

To those in need, I'll volunteer
before I'm asked (and be sincere).
When friends or family go astray,
I won't stand mute or look away.
Only fools will be ignored.
I won't waste time; I won't be bored.

Ecstatic just to be alive,
I'll nuzzle babies, plant high fives
on strangers' palms—for in this life
whatever has been out of whack
will effortlessly fall in line
like dominoes, when I come back.

In Paradise with Jane Austen

The psycholinguists call them "garden paths"—
those awkward sites of ambiguity
in sentences, where meaning bifurcates
so wantonly it stops us in our tracks,
leaving us at a loss which way to take.

Jane Austen never does this. Her deft prose
conducts us on a solitary path
whose fragrant nooks and arbors are designed
to fill the senses as her discourse flows
toward some hidden clearing of the mind:

a landscape of intelligence to match
one's deepest need; communion from which all
the nuisance of uncertainty is purged—
with every footstep measured, every hedge
articulated with uncommon love.

Lake Michigan Inlet

Its ripples strum the banks of grassy dunes,
where kids prance in a passing jet ski's wake.
Cooling your feet on summer afternoons,

you try to picture prehistoric Junes—
the glacial force, the eons it must take
for ripples to strum the banks of grassy dunes—

until the echolalia of the loons
reminds you that some truths are too opaque.
Just cool your feet. On summer afternoons

this blue, a kindred blueness in you swoons;
the only thing to do is to partake
in ripples that strum the banks of grassy dunes

and enter—by raft, yacht, kayak, pontoon—
a basin wide enough to quench your ache
or cool your feet on summer afternoons.

A simple beauty, common as the moon's,
attracts us to the shoals of this Great Lake,
whose ripples strum the banks of grassy dunes
and cool the feet on summer afternoons.

Knots

My yoga teacher, seeing me struggle,
   grabs the suspension ropes
      out of my hands,
      reweaves the strands,
and gives them back. I'm past all hope
of mastering the art of knots,
   apart from a bow or shoes—
      a shame, since they're
      used everywhere.
A feature on this morning's news
told how, in Palo Alto labs,
   cross-eyed microchemists
      with tiny tools
      tie molecules
in knots—a breakthrough, arguably premised
on the fumblings of inquisitive apes,
   whose pretzeled palm-frond hoops
      have wound their way
      through time's crochet.
In chromosomal feedback loops
it's handed down, the lore of knots.
   Phoenicians threading the seas
      with lanyards taut;
      starvations fought
with fishnets; hammocks; tapestries
all holding civilizations together.
   My husband now gets pissed
      when he can't pry
      a skewed bowtie;
he curses whatever step he's missed
in a proper knotter's preparation.
   Then there's me: on a sailboat with Dad,
      I'll see defeat
      in every cleat—

and though he tries not to get mad
(showing me how a bowline's rigged)
    we both get tied in knots.
        No one equips
        relationships
with handbooks for untangling clots.
That's the beauty of knots: they curve and close
    predictably on themselves,
        keeping things snug—
        till one quick tug
pulls them apart. The more one delves
into their intricacies (I think,
    while hanging upside down
        in yoga class—
        how time has passed!),
the more their elegance astounds.
Even if you're a klutz at knots
    like me, you're bound to find
        that well-closed curves
        can touch a nerve
in any loosely fastened mind.

The Chef at Home

He bakes with love. The extra care it takes
to blend two flours for a flawless crumb,
enriches every layer of his cakes.
His pie crusts, crimped with forefinger and thumb,
are brushed with egg to gleam like Aztec gold.
Banana bread—each slice a perfect sponge
for tea—he'll make on mornings when it's cold,
while evenings end with the unseemly plunge
of forks through cheesecake. Guests come to be primed
for heaven by the scent of his soufflé,
which tastes like friendship warmed. And once it's time
to brown the custard skins of crème brûlée,
the sugar crystals show no signs of scorch—
turning to caramel under his blue torch.

The Night We Put Tchaikovsky On

The night we put Tchaikovsky on
and sank into our seats
behind the windshield of a boat that crawled
along the dank Milwaukee River
under vaulted, grillwork streets,

it seemed to fill all crevices
with sympathetic sound.
The moaning resonance of violins
among the oil-brindled barges
that we carved a path around

made every cavity stand out:
pockmarks in the hull
where sewage gushed from puckered spouts;
the hold from which a crane unloaded
cargo on its tentacle.

A wind picked up that seemed to fit
a swelling in the brass.
Through churned debris we turned our MasterCraft
sharp at a pivoting railway bridge,
admiring its iron truss.

The waste refinery discharged
a smell like diesel gas,
and moonlit silos—emptied of their grain—
grew mammoth as we neared them, brushed
by silhouettes of wild grass.

We nestled in the boat that night
more sure of where we were.
An eastern front had blown the clouds away,
bringing to light a speckled sky
and waters more particular.

Groom's Song

Show me, love, where daffodils
are sweetening the breeze
while waving to the cool green hills
their silky, scented sleeves.

Share with me the first June rose
whose layers, as they spread,
reveal how gradually life grows
complex and fiery red.

At harvest, bring chrysanthemums
to match our autumn mood.
We'll face whatever hardship comes
with copper fortitude.

And when the spiny evergreens
are bent with snow—just then,
lean closer, promise me we'll see
the daffodils again.

About the Author

David Southward grew up in southwest Florida and earned degrees in English from Northwestern University (BA '90) and Yale (PhD '97). Since 1998 he has taught literature, film, and comics in the Honors College at the University of Wisconsin-Milwaukee. His chapbook, *Apocrypha* (Wipf & Stock 2018), reimagines scenes from the life of Jesus in a series of sonnets. In 2017 he was awarded the Lorine Niedecker Prize from the Council for Wisconsin Writers (selected by Tyehimba Jess) and the Muse Prize from the Wisconsin Fellowship of Poets; his poem "Mary's Visit" won the 2019 Frost Farm Prize for Metrical Poetry. A resident of Milwaukee, David enjoys cooking, gardening, and traveling with his husband, Geoff. Read more at davidsouthward.com.

www.ingramcontent.com/pod-product-compliance
Lightning Source LLC
Chambersburg PA
CBHW031000090426
42737CB00007B/610